Dus kahaniyaan

Clever Fox
PUBLISHING

Chennai • Bangalore

Dus kahaniyaan

Max K

ISBN:

Published by CLEVER FOX PUBLISHING

Table of Contents

One

Can this be changed!

Herons formulae, Pythagoras theorem, *alpha's* son *beta*, and his mom Mrs. *gamma*!

There exists an other long lasting family who is still balancing there life since old decades and here they are, *sin theta* who was once in young love with *cos theta,* and soon after 9 months they had cute little baby boy called *tan theta. Cosec theta* was the sister of *sin theta*, the most funniest guy in the *theta* family and the other members were nearly shipped from the other parts of the cosmic world. The long term disturber Mr Darwin, who had nearly made 10th life the *sabzi* of doldrums and blahs! The contraceptives acts were always engrossing with the most doubts but wirra! The saddened folk tales of French revolution and the long revolts always baffled me with the cries.

C' Mon! The **history** can't be dealt too much. Lok Sabha and Rajya Sabha had its all different logic that my mind couldn't reciprocate it. *Tataara vaamiro katha,* was an inspiring love story in which the hero pulls out his nerve power to break the land into two pieces with a fucking wooden sword, well this science of reasoning is out of the era at the moment; though the other way lust in the chapter nearly saved my interest in subject *hindi.* Now the thing *comes to* fiftyish, bald head *hamare patol babu (our patol babu)* who made us learn the true value of teacher and the true dedication towards your work. According to me, I'm still not able to understand the chemistry of my life and will be neither, apart from this I was not able to solve the real hard core chemistry where calculating the moles was a different level of frustration and balancing the equation was the other disheartenment.

Do you know? There exists an another traditional family consisting of, *proton* who is always spooked up and sits in the core, who always spends time and tide with neutron, and the *electron* who literally do not cares what's going on and keeps revolving.

It feels crap to study this all, and looking at nerds who just never had a true interest in study but kept running behind the teacher even when the class got over, just to make others look towards them and to add extra cheese burst to the teacher with the benefit of marks. These geeks are nearly the front benchers, who dress like *maharajas* and they sit like it too; ask simple questions so they are certified by the teachers that they are showing much interest. The back benchers are always cool, they spend their time doodling on tables like ______ love ______., and making moustaches and beards on cartoon sketches of political science book. Apart from this, we see studs or pro who start making love at the last bench. They always have a different identity, which is not required to be specified. Erasers were always being hit, and paper bomb, pen fights made the school life somehow more riveting. Centre fresh or boomer sticky bomb was always glued below the table. Our English teacher was the most bony lady in the entire school, and her period was meant to be most awaited, everyday a new dress on her could be expected. On the other hand our maths teacher with a 6'2 feet height, who always had his one finger near his ginger looking nose. We usually had his period after the lunch break and believe me, then there were no lullabies required, the only thing what used to fit into our mind at that moment was a good sleep. All the formulas were nearly evaporated after his period and I had to somehow condense those before the exams. I became *murga (cock)* in the class twice in my life and that was something which I could never forget. Well, I have been behind the principal office room for some crazy love things. I always tried to cry at that moment, but anyways god didn't gift me the art of crying and the moment I try to cry, I tend to make some weird emotions where I allow others to be sad and happy at the same time. What do I call this act? WEIRD OR VERY WEIRD!

See, there are always two reasons behind of you being called in the principal's office room. One reason is that you might have done really good in something and the other is you might have flown out some blood of your enemy's nose or you might have ended up being caught in some crazy love trap scene. My ratio of being called in principal's office was more inclined towards the love trap thing.

Hey! Sorry I forgot to introduce, I'm Max, a typical *desi* guy, loves gyming but never had a record to do it more than two months; figuring out the food I love, it changes over time like u change your girl. I'm 18 and just have completed my 10th grade hopefully. I have a good hand on piano and loves to write what others do not, kind of philosophical. I have a dinky ....no! not that hopefully . . . .

I have a small cute rabbit (Bunny) who always swipes his tongue over my hand; he loves me so much, that even my future wife wouldn't afford to. Spinach, wheat, banana, cauliflower leaves, and sometimes coriander is what all he affords to stuff in his stomach. Normally he dealt with my three charger's wire, all broken. Now I always keep it out of his reach, so my phone is not dead. When there is no one to except my shit, he is always running around me with his pink ears uncurving. He hides behind my room's cupboards and technically plays *luka chupi* (hide and seek). Always a fun time with him.

Two

How about being a Dropout

It was a dilatory night, the stars winkle so I do wanted to, dreamt to get my light through many of the atmospheric refraction layers so that humans leering me downstairs watch my apparent position. I wanted to be at a secret position in the skin of the earth and maybe that's what I always wanted. The woeful truth behind the bars would crumble the history; the spell was in the kitchen and once this hex works, the world would be alike a sweet pixie. I will become a mega star and ogle downstairs, the small things over bleak sky. Something will change and flutter the present watch, future will be unclear mist of flurry snow and the past nothing to talk about it.

It all started yeah! I dropped the school after my 10th examination! FUCKK! I did this, I seriously fucking DROPPED the school like dope.

I didn't wait for the results, because I knew it would kick my ass harder, and would have tried to kill myself after seeing the result book. Moreover I tried to cook some lame excuses for my engineer minded relative that usually never worked out in real.

Still dreaming to see my crowd at a big arena with the swinging flashlights and good smile. Imagine, thousands of flashlights waving in front of you; how would you reciprocate? Stars over the ground?

I never follow people because every time I feel so following them I end up making some beautiful shit! Long back when I was 4 years old small boy, I used to walk with some sound baking shoes. It used to make some crazy sounds that ended me up to walk more. Everyone around used to see me because of the shoes and my baby florid outfits. My mom used to take me for the piano lesson on rickshaw which I hardly did that a month. My father was a singer and is a production manager at ply wood factory.

I was born in a middle class family and never felt its drawback till I was somewhere around 16. After 14, I was inspired by some of the lionized stars like chain smokers, lost stories. So here I was, a dropout and was taking some professional music production courses, in one of the good colleges of Mumbai.

My fathers eyes were big round, and it felt that they were going to be dropped from his eye shell when he heard me talking about something called being a dropout, and I can feel them being dropped when I actually dropped off.

Landing to *Bombay,* was like a dream coming true. Buildings here are so tall that you might end up overstretching your neck sometimes. Here you may spot one of the richest men and on the parallel, one the poorest.

No one here gives a damn sweet shit about anyone. Mumbaikers know almost everything, they actually do miracle when they use the water so efficiently by running their daily work in a bucket or so. They whizz through the local trains as if the scenario is, when your house has a single washroom and relatives have come to your house, and moreover everyone is waiting and looking at the washroom door without there eyes being clicked.

I travel everyday from *dadar to chembur* for the music production courses and yeah I have to run down my ass through a huge public and always keep my phone and goggles safe as they are the only two things in my life that I bought more than 5 times, and I didn't want to loose them again.

I don't know if this is the case with everyone or just dumbs like me but it usually happens with me

At a pan shop, *dadar.*

"Bhaiya! Which bus will go to chembur?" I asked him heavily, because u ought to have confidence in Mumbai.

"Bus no. 376!" He said with perfection and I asked him twice because I went to the wrong bus thrice this week. He switches his ritualized *agarbatti* (incense stick) and I fetch myself to the bus stop.

I still have good hopes in my pocket mixed with some solid dilemmas and there I wait at the bus stop for around half an hour and to my luck, I found the treasure, the bus no. 376.

I got into it, and headed toward the half bald headed conductor. He wore the old round glasses and his sagacious looks made him look better.

"*One single ticket for chembur!*" I said him confidently

He held his still face for a second and finally dropped down his sweet words.

"The bus won't go to *chembur*"

So, this was the fourth time I falsified myself and got down at the next stop.

Sometimes life Fu*** you like never before; you need to borrow euphoria from someone but eventually you always end up lending your happiness to someone, and feel so dampen then.

Life was merely flipped up. Its hard to manage everything so suddenly when you leave your house and start managing your own things. You have to pretty much figure out everything, from money to food and then food to your health. I turned up getting sick three times in a month, so yeah it becomes hard to settle down everything. You don't live in those regular home time table, you need to make your own new time table of life once you leave your family and house temporarily. Priorities and almost everything gets changed. You try to explore world, let other people come into your life, and then finally you start getting matured!

Never underestimate a dropout. Being a dropout is one of the biggest risks in life and you must have a thick ass for it. You are always allowed to live the way ***you*** always want to, not the way ***they*** always want to. ***So yeah, live the way you love.***

Three

Marvels of Travel

Sir! Taxi, *kaha sir bandra!, boss taxi?,Bhaiya cab?, chaii! Chaii! Kafee! Kafee! Dost! Where? Kuthe zaycha aahe? (in Marathi language) linking road? Bolo na sir kidhar jaoge, aaiye sir kaha jaoge, taxi?, kaha jaoge sir?*

I personally feel like to fit a punch to their face and ask them to ask me once again for the ride to their city. They just sit on you until you say no or *nahi chaiye Bhaiya.* Sometimes they behave like they are far better than the local paid tourist guys and they know inside out of the city and this maybe real.

This is how a travel journey embarks on; you come out of the railway station and you are already greeted with the taxi or the auto drivers before your relatives of the city. Nowadays I feel even the cab drivers are in better pants than me. But gone are the days when we used to show some sympathy towards auto drivers. Taking Uber or OLA is in the fashion and it updates your status. Just a few length of minutes and you get the bio of your driver and no fucks is given to the auto nowadays. I do still love those old three seater ride with plush seats, alongside the free AC of the nature. Captions behind the autos are damn cool!, they are like *has mat pagli pyaar hojayega . . . . . hum do hamare do. . . . . .*You can see these behind the bigger trucks too which are driven by drunk truck pilots. ***This is the marvel of my India; travel and then see the trucks when you are unemployed and hide your smile back.***

Have you seen overpopulated autos with one guy hanging with his half ass along with the driver? LMAO! The share autos have an other side of fun.

"Monday has been officially cancelled." Shrey said dropping his morning bread down

"I mean why, are you skipping your office today?" I replied him back

Mondays blues are so in vogue and the coffee gives me the best solution. Nucleya's (Indian DJ) track have always perked up my weekdays. For the first time I played his track over the loud, I jumped over the bed twice on the drop and barely cared about anything else, like the burning of rice over the stove. Music actually affiliates me to the Venus; senses me all far than a planet. The whole nine yards turns off when it comes to electronic dance music.

Sun was glimmering brighter than yesterday. Well, Mondays are supposed to be powerful according to the almighty. Rain was over the city since last week and haply today the sun must have collaborated with the heavy clouds to bring something new.

"Bhai, coffee?" I asked Shrey as he takes his bread and jam

"Half cup, three sugar spoons!" He says and sits at the couch that we could only afford for a one room space.

I take the coffee mugs and sit besides him and ask about the Monday cancelation thing. Cold morning of monsoon and a mug of coffee makes the day.

"Pack your suitcase." Shrey says as he gulps his coffee

"Bhai, are you out of the Sunday hangover?" I asked him as he normally says irrelevant things sometimes and then regret it later.

"I ain't joking brat." he says. Brat was now his well established word on me. I take the cigarette pack and share with Shrey.

"What's the new plan? And why do you remind yourself of this on Monday?" I asked him, lightning up the cigarettes.

"A Road trip to Nainital" he says after shooting a drag.

"Bc, that's around 300 km ride from Delhi" I raised my eyebrows.

"As if I did not know it ahead of." He says and slides of his office bag.

"Is everything fine?" I asked looking directly to him.

"No bro, I want a 3 day off from this job, I need a break now; so fucked up of this routine." he says, crashing his cigarette butts over the ash tray. He looked fitful and uneasy; he was all good the previous day, and had good time in the Hauz

Khaz last night, though the drinks were highly priced but the money was never a issue with him. Beer stock was never out in our fridge.

A minute later.

"You are right though" I sighed and kept my mug aside.

Crows pushed their interlude to our conversation and our roadside pet *billi* sneaked through the window. The cold soil beside our house was fresh and added a good odour to the room. I looked at the dried crisp leaves at the balcony, all broken with the cloth of yellow. Sometimes the dried ones look better, it matches the status of our life, all broken, shattered and fractured. Cooker whistles were blown after a minute and I went back to the kitchen. Slow mornings and the half shut eyes. I carried out my everyday ritual of feeding the milk to cat and defined this as my true love.

"What are you waiting for, Shrey, pack your bags!" I said him with my longest possible voice that reached over the whistle of cooker.

I looked myself in mirror figuring out my pimples and dark spots. Pimples behave like *bin bulaye mehmaan* (***guests who were never called***) and these type of guests never leave and mark the spot behind. And this summer they have overgrown without a reason. Never mind, the point is to find beauty in everything. Its just the way how you think upon. It must be around two decades I have been looking for myself over the glass. You see your ghost in front of you, doing stuffs that you are on too. A glass can help to figure out, who you really are, tall, thin, fat, fucked up, depressed, happy etc. and it charges nothing to tell you, gives free true report everyday. How helpful! Imagine a world without mirrors! Well, I wouldn't be aware of my pimples, and ***Dakota Johnson*** wouldn't know about her beauty till date.

"Bhai, you alive or you started day dreaming before we started the trip." he nearly screamed and was seeming happy though.

What else then! Aloo bhujia, Bourbon, cup cakes, Lays, Kurkure, candies, chocolates, marshmallow were kept aside and packed. I have been dating aloo bhujia since a decade now, and still not bored of its taste. Britannia had been all times favourite, my mom used to give me after the school hours but Oreo had overtaken it now. Some tea packets, cigarettes, lighters, knife, apples were kept along. Ripped T shirts and jeans are the best attire I feel to wear. Tracksuits, Nike sneakers and some mufflers were the other things to wrapped.

After reaching Nainital.

Street maggi made my eyes upon. I caught the beautiful aroma of the 2 min Maggi, the best hunger defeater in the universe. There might be no one who haven't tasted these yellow spirals with good soup. Years before this was the alternative for my breakfast but soon it changed to lunch and dinner. This taste of addictiveness is like an endless circle, a ***big round circle.***

Resort - The Fern

We were resting over the cold fat mattresses with the best pillows I would have ever slept upon, sipping the hot Earl green Himalayan tea and charging ourselves with the best unsmoked natural breeze. At a point in a life you need to freed yourselves from all the responsibilities you are tied with and the one you are stitched along. You feel yourself a prominent character in someone's life after taking the responsibility. A time arrives where we do not try to feel responsible for ourselves but tend to feel for others. We get glued under the cobwebs of other's life and then never feel to get out after adapting into it. We finally got the time to release ourselves and the stress tried to lower itself like the domino effect. It was a state of solitude, all still, none of us bared to converse along and sipped the tea with ease.

Never get too locked in the society, if so, then find a key and try to unshackle yourself for a moment. Dig deep and find yourself, the muffled you, and take a long breath. ***Awake yourself before it dies.*** When you find it, the life gets better in an another way. Sometimes you never know what exactly you are. It doesn't add a tax to locate your soul, it makes your life easier and dumps all the scariness of the life. Sometimes the life is more fazed and mystified like the unsolved cube toy. You never know which step is needed to be taken first to make your cube perfect with all colours. The answer to this mystifying situation is to just pull your inner self from the deep well which is intoxicated with all the world poops. The normal timeline of a person of this century deals from his/her school's homework then the teenage problems, then finally comes the stack of college books and beers, a later on brings the beautiful girl/boy for a proposal and then the time comes to wash your kids ass. Old age is the time to rest yourself with all the diseases and tablets the world could ever process along and you see your kids growing and frowning up. Life runs on medicines then and the chapter closes ploddingly. We bring ourselves to this earth and looses soon without even knowing ourselves. Strange huh? Well yeah.

"Kaha le aya bhai?" 9 (Where did you bring me dude!) I asked him after sipping my last sip.

"Why? Are you enjoying?"

"Well, Sherry you make sense in terms of making quick plans!" I complimented him after a long time.

"Rehende bhai, ghee bachale." he smiled back.

Short conversations over quick bites made the day healthier. Evening sun shone through the window spaces. I recalled the Tindal effect after I saw the straight rays. Pretty good old 10th physics class. Did you remember we were supposed to stress on the fucking convex and concave mirror diagrams without a reason and calculating the position of image, object and it's magnification. Seriously? Am I gonna take the convex lens out in the world and check for its position of image. Hell No! I remember how I used to scratch my head when the formulas in the light chapter never worked out in my notebook and in real life. Well, it's completely subjective, some of the kids liked to rotate their head in the diagrams and formulas.

So Nainital is quite a good tourist place where you enjoy it's sweet corn with different *masalas,* long big momos in the last corner of the famous shopping lane (if anyone has visited Nainital) and rolling your tongue over ice cream is one of the best experience here .

"Whoa! Look at those yachts." Shrey pointed to the lake

"Yeah, they look amazing, independent and bright." I said with my soft voice.

A life is all about taking breaks and exploring the way you like it. One of the most common phrase these days, over taking breaks and exploring is "I need a six month holiday twice a year".

I wish the phrase to take over the real life. Its all about what, where, and how you explore anything, and that may be yourself. Once you explore yourself in and out, the things start to fall in place.

"When are we leaving by the way?" Shrey questioned me.

I swipe my fingers through my long sleek hair and adjust them. I gave a short look to Shrey and said

"This was one of the best short trip ever, thanks bro"

"I appreciate your words." He said while winking me back.

Millions of us travel everyday to make our family rapturous or to earn few more bucks down the town. We travel to release endorphins, and to be tired, we travel to date someone or to meet near the dark corner place. We have different perceptions to travel, some have lots of wonga and clothes to wander around without checking the clock. Some travel to talk with the Himalayas, to bath in holy rivers, to go for a nature walk or to photograph their own bae. Bouquet of reasons to travel and flock around. We travel everyday on an average, well not an statement for the play station lovers but yeah they do travel, room to room. We sweep through the different cultures round the world, different languages, different seasons and what not, variance booties, odd cuisine with some cute looking ***desert*** on a big plate. We see mini black yellow cab in Mumbai, some decorative ***tuk tuk*** (auto) around the India which are overloaded but the driver still adjusts to fit his hands on the accelerator with a *ghutkha in his mouth.* Bright yellow painted cabs of Kolkata, that usually fits in frames of many travellers, and then traveling in thin lanes of *chandni chowk* on the slanted rickshaws in Delhi is another type of fun. There's lot to explore, lot to travel – a life itself is a travel. Even though you don't wish to travel, life makes you travel from day to other day.

We feel high as a kite when board examinations finally gets over and get some time to travel and reach out better place. It makes us to travel practically rather than traveling in an imaginary way with sin and cos theta in the school rooms. We feel responsible when we travel, we feel independent, enjoy, care ourselves and feel better without any much aid. Sometime a travel can make a delight in someone's life, never know it can be a beautiful wife with eyes full of treasures and heart as big as kingdom. A travel can carry you to the Mars too, a travel can take you undersea, or let's say over the Everest, near the Eiffel's tower, and endless.

What about when you go for skydiving and row through the winds with the shower of cries and smiles!

There's lot to travel, there's lot to explore, lot to wander.

Sometimes we travel because of emergency, we travel when someone turns up dead, or move when someone is on the verge of dying, travel to save someone's magical life, travel when someone is dead due to accident to lend some help, or when someone's under the weather.

A wave of strangeness though when we think why do we and how important it turns to be to travel around the day. It could turn to one of the best or the worst experience. *A very common phrase, every coin has 2 sides.*

Four

Burst of Lust

(Just an imagination, this just never happened)

The door was pimpled with the rusty shade, pumping somewhere it's grand vintage look and nimbu mirchi was the first thing I saw over the door. They say the ghosts never flock around when you hang the lemons this way. I mean why? Do the ghost hate lemons.

Wait! Now can you figure out that how does a *single mirchi looks with two lemon on the either side?*

Instagram notification

Kritika- Where are you?

Me - On the doorstep!

Kritika – Oh, gimme a couple of minutes.

And that's been running since past evening. I have broken the world record for the fastest dating. Even the tinder couldn't afford the lustiness I prefer, and I feel the *tharak* (Lust) inside her. So probably fixing the best date in my life right now. I ain't sure about the steps taken in my life, never felt confident for the steps I have taken but the thing is I never regret what I have done in the past. I wish, after I meet her, I do not regret anything in the future.

Waiting for the door to open! I adjust my round frames perfectly and shape the hair through the glass of the window. I wore a classic black polo T shirt on a cream chinos and overspread the FOGG this time. I am obsessed with its old commercial and now with its new one this time. Its like, a guy turns up and says

"Kya chal raha hai?"

And the other guy sneaks in and says,

"Fogg chal raha hai!"

This was as cool as the backbenchers treat the teacher, especially when it comes to Hindi classes. The 5 star advertisement made its own place over the one of the most liked ads. Ramesh!! Suresh!!!

The door creeks slowly and she opens it with her coffee mug in the hand. She wore a skirt and an off shoulder with a light makeup. A black small *bindi* what she wore made her more appealing than yesterday. She smiles wide, adjusts her hair and welcomes me in. I take my shoes off and walk in. Her living room was alike the reception of a 5 star residency. Flowers case round the corner, aquarium with no fishes inside, masterpiece was hung over the wall and the clock of grandparent's arena was right above the smart TV. There I found a *diwan* at the left side of the room where I wished to take my ass down.

"Chill! Mom isn't at home" she says, dropping her coffee mug at the table

"Why do I need your mom?"

"*Areeh!* I mean we can chill around"

For sure; I kept those words inside me.

(*It all begin yesterday 17th July, 2019, at the evening near the hanuman temple of the society where I lived. The mosquitoes began their usual work of sucking and hovering over the head. Seeing the mosquitoes I start to think of my old friends who feel free to itch me anytime. The lamp near the temple kept itself in confusion and turned off eventually. I was back from the cycle ride after a long time and figured my gears stuck in the middle of my way. I took a bent and after switching on my phone's flash-light I found that the gear box was completely fucked up. No!! This was the second time my cycle was behaving in a weird way.*

I saw a shadow and felt someone was coming towards me, a feel of conjuring was on my mind. I tilted my head over and saw a girl outfitted in the gym clothes. She comes down towards me.

I haven never looked so good, so that the girl comes directly towards me, but this was some different case. No! She did not look like Sharma ji's nor Agarwal ji's beti, she looked something out of the city.

"May I help you?" she asks politely

"Well, thank you, the cycle is totally fucked up" I got up from my bent over position.

"Lemme check!" she says.

I mean why she figured out to repair my cycle. I thought over and swiped my sweat. This did not looked normal for me, technically not for me.

A minute later.

"Dude its really a mess with the gear box." she says and clears her throat.

She checked the cycle and left her ass to be glanced by me, and I am a kind of ***tharki*** *the world could ever find. She bent and checked the cycle for a long now. A girl haven't gifted me a chocolate ever and she is craving to check my cycle over. This would never sound real, it will sound reel.*

"Yay! I think the mechanic is helpful now."

She cleans her black oily hand of what the chain did and I just kept staring her.

"Well, thanks." I had to say though

"No, problem. I have seen you around. Do you stay here?"

"Umm, yeah, A- block 408"

"That's cool, I just stay opposite to your building; B block" she gives a vague smile and slides her coffee hair.

"Can we move towards the building, it's so dark down here." she says, sipping her diet coke

Why dude?? Why she looks so interesting? (A thought of moment)

We exchanged the random introduction which a normal girl and a boy of eighteen could have. It lasted for half an hour and I figured out the right girl this time. I kept staring at the diet coke can and thought she would share a sip. The main thing we did was we exchanged Instagram accounts and were over the truth dare game the full night we met. The dares turned out to be like kiss me, buy me chocolate, propose me and blahs!. It turned out to be my best truth dare of the millennium. This all was screening like Karan Johar's movie scenes now, imaginary and true.

This was all common for me, I was a born flirt and ***tharki,*** *but things were turning out real this time and my faith was still alive; not alike in the scenarios of catching the wrong bus. It takes no fucking time to switch the situation and I'll tell you know how, it's like you never think of a girl and the next moment she repairs your cycle; you never think of a faster zomato delivery and the boy arrives at the doorstep with the confusion of change and this has always been my hook line.*

"Bhaiya 500 ka change hai kya?" (bro do you have a change of 500rs)

And the answer is always familiar as of girls rejection.

"Nai hai sir." (No I do not!)

Every shit happens for a good but there's another level of controversy that why does some shit sound bad. Does that bad shit is a good shit, or there's everything good in our life and nothing bad.)

She arrives with a tray and a glass of water. She drops the tray down the table and lets her cleavage to be viewed clearly and this sounded like an American pie now. She sat next to me on the diwan and sighed with a relief and checked her Snapchat doggy filters.

"*Pav bhaji or samosa*?" she asked after she sat next to me.

Was her fogg more stronger than me or was it mines which was reciprocating to me.?

"Coke will be fine now." I said to her

"Dumb! I asked about the snack now."

"Um. A Samosa with a red *chutney."* I had to say as she offered it quite politely to me.

"Wait I'll get it you." she gets up to the kitchen

She drops herself back in a minute with the crispy samosas and the chutney. Her black *bindi* was officially making her *rani* and she was so curvy.

I haven't seen curves like her, I mean never.

Samosas were from the *Gupta ji's* shop and let me tell you, his samosa's are the most consumed snack in this society. If I am ever invited to someone's house for a get together, *Gupta ji ke* samose are must. Her house was one of the best neatly kept house I have ever visited. If you ever visit to my house, my jockey would be hanging around the corner, and some used tissue around. Being hygienic is one of the toughest job I feel. If you ask me how many times I bath in a week, my answer would be around 3 times. Well, yeah! That's too unhygienic.

"So, Vikram, How's life?" she asked me

"It's good, and I think it turned better after these samosas!" I sighed back

"Just with those samosas?" she raises her eyebrows

"Yeah and I think its turning better after talking with you!"

"Hittin' me!" she slightly raised her voice

"Yeah! Just started to." I gave a short smile.

She patted me and giggled a bit while sliding her hair back. We played the truth dare last night and I thought she must have canned those dare the last night itself. It happens a lot, you chat something different, then you talk and act something nearly opposite to what you chat in your real life. Snapchat and Instagram had made the life much easier and faster but less interactive though. I nearly called all my senses out just to check her half -suppressed smile and the eyes. A silence of few seconds, that might take an autumn leaf to fall over was passed. I clear out my throat and kept the plate aside.

"So! Should we turn those dares into reality?" I asked her with a confidence that is usually carried by a small kid.

Oh Kriti! We did it. The overlapping *dhak dhak* of our hearts was uncontrollable, nothing was stable. The dopamine was released and resolved with the blood. The way we say *chai main ghooli chinni (sugar mixed in the tea).*

"Ugh! Don't bite my lips" I said to her after a minute of gap

"I ain't" she says and plays with my hair. I haven't thought over the wilderness of a girl can show up. I was not able to take myself; my hands started to cup her ass and the moans were rhythmically heard now.

"Are we doing right?" I asked while kissing her neck.

"There's no rule to live the world." she says with an another moan

She says right though. I have been living my life after rules and was too tired of it. Follow this! Do that! Come home before 7! Eat on time! Bath on time else mom is always behind with a stick! Study! Sleep! Blahs and so many fucks in life.

Nothing in life felt important to me, all rules to be followed were evaporated now. The next day I had my preboards for maths and I was a ***blank*** like every time. Eyes were shut, everything was black but still it was an another level of trip. I slowly slid my hands all over her neck, she smiles a bit and moves her body. You never know what life makes you to do sometimes. All seclusion, no thoughts were grooving in my head, everything was finished, just the moment was to be cherished. I felt like winging in the air with no parachutes of backup and thought of been migrating to the other galaxy was at the moment. The hormones weren't at the controlled stage, all overloaded.

She moans and I glide my fingers around her blonde hair, ploddingly and it was the smack of Swarga. She pulled me down by the shirt, her lipstick was shading more smacks to my breaths, the uncontrollably poison of love was wafted between our eyes, and everywhere. We slowly moved down to the bed after diwan; I was unshaven that messed up my look, though making me sexier. She was slowly moving down her hands to my body. My heart was tapping the informal playlist of music and down my denim something was being popped out by some force. She began to strip off with the complete teasing looks. Her cat green eyes were spotted less than her high thighs. The cream of her body were longing to taste once, the seraphic made girl. Ouch!

I held her face and kissed her more.We kissed passionately, the noise of our striking tongues could be audible to those love birds in the vintage cage. Our lips got wet, but the saliva was like abetment for us. The gentle lips gifted us with an ostentatious feel that was like smooth music for us. Our breaths slowly got louder, in a vague crescendo. The sounds that came were savoury and luscious, holding us in waves of hedonism.

Our lips got a tad redder. Eyes were closed, and the other senses were diffused in the air like a cloud. It was light, calm, and tender touch of something what I was always craving for so long.

I was adept in kissing. I knew just when to move the tongue, when to make the sound and when to sandwich the female upper lip between our both. But I could notice she wasn't a rookie. She had kissed before. Naturally.

We were on it for quite some time, and only a maddening cough succeeded in ending our public pursuit of pleasure.

We huffed, and did not look at each other or anyone else for some time.

I was so HAPPY. I wanted to laugh my throat out. This kiss was the best I had ever done. Though maybe because this was the hottest girl I had kissed yet.

But it was merely the lust. It was a deep touch of her pinkish lips. It was something deeper. I knew it was. I was dumbfound. I was always 'not committed enough'. I didn't WANT to be. I liked refashion.

But Kritika was different. I didn't want to lose her. I wanted this relationship to go on for long. I cupped my hands to her high thigh, and made ourselves more private area. Curtains flapped over and the door was shut with a wham. Brisk cold zephyr blew through the windows and it smelled of rain. After a five minute loop of wind, rain gave its *darshan,* and luckily this was the first shower of the season.

"Our lustness made the god to shower us with rain." she laughs

"That's the reason of pure lust." I say with a sharp voice.

"Whoop!" She shouts and unzips my jeans

I slowly crossed her honey blonde tail, the downy touch that made my heart pump from vertical to horizontal. The clock ticks were hazy after the soft moans. Her hairs were confessed up in the heavy maze, they were like body guarding the face. There was a special fire in her green eyes, a fire that was lit by my matchstick.

"Let me burn with you tonight." she said softly

"You need a matchstick." I laughed

The trade of afternoon was now hotter than ever, the libido mizzled up like champagne, and the kisses were kissed frequently like tequila shots.

After few minutes when then wind turned out with its breaks.

"Vikram! Was that a reverie?" she asks while handling her long hair

"My full life's been a fantasy when you came up." I stated with a pause

"Why doesn't it sounds real!"

"Because your lips are magical, it feels alike nothing else comforts me more."

"Why though?"

"Simple. *Because your lips have magic and the spell lies with me!*"

"I wanna loose myself." she says and cups my face

"And then what!" I said and pulled her sensitive soft waist towards me

"Twine with your subconscious mind so you never loose me" she unlaces her top hurriedly and looks at me

"Wish that happens!" I said her back

"*Kehte hai agar kisi cheez ko dil se chaho to puri kayanat usey tumse milane ki koshish main lag jatti hai"(**When you really desire something from the heart and soul, all the universe conspires you to achieve it**"*) *she purrs to my ears. Thanks to Paulo Coelho for the quote.*

"Never saw a female Shahrukh Khan though!" I answered and nuzzled her back

She wore an attractive red bra and and the tits were pounding off. I haven't seen a girl half nude just in front of me and probably doing things what I always wanted to do. No! Either the time should stop and rewind or we should freeze the activity we are into. Chimes played its own music of infinite phrases. Love birds might have begun their own way of pleasurable work. Bedsheets were half removed, pillows were thrown down, curtains were slammed, door was locked and lights were shut.

"***Ride me like never before"*** she says in a hushed tone

Five

Unknown Concepts

Balloons

(In this chapter, Ashish, an upper middle class guy wanders around the city and finds something weird with balloons)

He just came out of the café, walked down the local streets, with the air like comfy bin and whiff of like late night club was still alive. Babies were spotted down with the baby-sitter who expressed themselves as the baby batman or spider man while sitting out on that snug sitter. They were driven by their mom with the sweet milk in the bottle. Caring about the baby is a major issue, holy it irritates sometimes. Nowadays the kids are so matured that they start falling in love at the age of 8 itself. The peace of the boulevard was carried up by the street musician; they were like feeding love to the air, like we say adding an extra topping to your pizza so that it looks cuter often. The balloon sellers were marking their pockets with few dollars, which he really didn't like at all.

Balloons are something beyond belief; it makes your heart fill with better blood. When you hold up those vivid balloons, your heart's gardener sprinkles paint of happiness, the nakedness joy, and much more. These balls of air don't hold much in themselves but air, with a thin shade of colour to its cover, but if you see normal balloons they don't fly, they are just type of balls which you kick like your friends, they bounce up an and you can hold that better; talking about the helium figured balloon, which is a balloon in itself but it flies high, kisses the clouds, flirts with air, and enjoys. So, the whole extract is, what really matter is what stuff is inside you, is it normal air or helium gas. Who you really are?

A normal balloon that deflates after few day or a helium filled one that flies up at the special events, and rises and rises till it reaches out of normal eyes. Settling away from the reach of normal eye can make you do anything.

This is what balloon teaches him; still the seller is paid with thin dollars. He just circled around the park and returned back to the hotel room that satisfied him at the last. By seeing the bed, he used to remember his mom's hug. When he drops himself down at the bed like jumping of the mountain, he usually gets the feel of kindliness of a hug.

He dove his mind to crackle up the quest, it was like a walnut, and door arms were needed to get those tasty nuts. He destined himself to hold a coffee to his hand, that look fancy sometimes with his cool boxer and a shirt at the balcony. He is fond of the atmosphere when its drunk away and often shoots up with bold looking cigars.

So the next time you get a balloon for yourself, pay the seller a few more extra coins and make him smile.

Men and Women

(Somewhere around the globe)

The breeze didn't turn calm since evening, it was dominating its power. The pong of black beans wafted out the coffee shop, clarinet played its own buzz, and the late night clubs bounced out its own hard rock, the bebop of 1940s was cultured by the drum and the trumpet at the cafe. The different taste of music made the perfect cuisine for me this night. My watch seemed to be sprinting along, my arms started tottering for the foremost time.

Look down, look up, look right, look left, you rotate around, what do you see?

I guess there are many things that spoil your minds, that feels you better, feel delectable, feel horny, feel up with the worsen mood, there are different perspectives of how do you see your ambiance and how you cook that shit in your mind, bull shit or good shit ?

I see everything, I take in every thought. Everywhere there is something out of the ordinary, it's all about how you take it. I gaze to people, well gazing them is not a long shot, but yeah, seeing chicas down the Paris with some of the sexiest figure gives an elite smell to my eye. I walk down to the various malls, short cropped roads with the relish of after rain.

What I am trying to say is that, all around the world, the city you live, the society you feed on, the house you live there is something marvel, and that is *people around you.* Just bring that thought on, get a couch, hold on to a coffee or wine and imagine; there are dissimilar people around you, all with altered faces, their structure is tailored differently from top to bottom. Bring that idea, how everyone could be so different, leave the twins issue aside, but, that's more than a miracle, everyone has different pizza base with their own flavoured cheese. Everything is different, look everyone, everyone has a different body shape and face; isn't that something eerie and wonderful, everyone looks different, it's attention-grabbing though, we can flirt with all the type of girls. This fact dips me into pool of curiosity that how everyone around me smells me different, what's the Fu****g power, is that a generator type of power, or something aircraft power, this puts me into another confusion, is that something related to god power, (I know everything is scientific nowadays but!!!). Well!! What if a twin boy and girl, marry up, and have baby, how will the baby look like. Ha-ha! tricky issues, that rushes your mind hard.

So the whole point is, enjoy living with everyone, you won't find the same person again in any corner of this world. Respect everyone and love them back. We are so great full to have millions of people around us. Different ones have different role out there. You yourself might have a different role.

So this sphere has people of different faces, character, and everything. If someone hates you there are others to love you. So, be calm and love everyone.

Roll dà coaster

Ohh! Woaahhhhhh!

This rollercoaster ride was much needed in my life. I was always a kilometre away from the rollercoaster ride corner and my friends, without a fail used to carry me towards it like the brisk wind carries almost everything.

See, its very very spine-tingling for me to be in the ride for few strange minutes of my life. Have you ever seen its structure? It's a fucking 7D model of a small intestine. And dude! Believe me once you are done with this ride, your mind will start spinning around. Never ask your photographs after the ride, because once you scan that photo, you will probably figure out your unreal emotions on your bewteful face.

At times when I am alone, these moments flash upon my inward eye and I burst out with some grin on my face.

A solo rollercoaster ride almost taught me everything much needed in my life. It taught me how the graph of life goes.

When u fasten your belt for the rollercoaster ride, you actually start the journey of your real life. Then the machine starts whistling and you start going forward. The ride proceeds in a smoother way for the initial seconds just as of your starting periods in life, where you are treated very carefully over snug bed. Then the rollercoaster shows its reality after taking small sharp curves. This depicts your life when you are around the age 10 and life tries to generate some problems. The ride maintains a good flow for a fruitful time and then it really inclines up in a semi circle to depict our teenage diaries where we boost our hormones, anger, happiness, sadness to a higher frequency level. Teenage years are supposed to be most happening years of life, you start growing matured, start maintaining crushes of your class and try getting high on drugs, smokes and alcohol for the first time. Physics NCERT and Rd Sharma start to behave like *bin bulaaye mehmaan.*

Life gets happier and is happy till the rollercoaster reaches the highest peak after inclining the huge curve.

3 . 2 . 1

And then neither the rollercoaster nor the life waits for anyone, it drops off so harsh from the cliff and we nearly loose all our senses. This is when we face the outcomes of all the bad things we did in our teenage days. We feel the hit in our life and decline so fast just as the rollercoaster does. After few days, we stabilize ourselves and go with a fresh start. This never takes a halt, the rollercoaster takes good sharp turns in your mid-30s, then maybe 50s, you may loose your job or you might get promoted to a big post. After some good 5 minutes, the rollercoaster ride brings itself to an end, just how life brings to. Everything takes a pause, you unbuckle yourself and life comes to an end. How relatable, huh!

Time

How unfettered do you feel now? Where are you? Has anyone hypnotised you? Are you free to fly? Do you wanna be the next star? Are you packed in a room? Do you wanna fly out together with someone?

We were kids with all those small little feet, watched the world with barely no brains. A pair of biscuit with the doraemon on the screen was the everyday thing. Modes of transportation were changed in a shorter period from crawling to the crawler then to the tricycle and finally on two legs. Crying over for candies and lollipops is what I still remember. Bed tales with the bournvita cup on the edge of my bed was the best package. Mum's stories used to end with a warm kiss over my forehead and I used to sleep comfortably wrapping myself inside the snug quilt. I carry a habit of talking during my sleep and that's bit weird. The next morning I used to wake up and my mom used to tell me all the talks I used to have in the sleep.

I used to be fascinated by looking at those small glittering gadgets called stars. Sometimes they drop by with a quick speed and I as always ask my secret wishes. My wishes were never fulfilled instead of few, but still asking for the wishes, that wouldn't be true carries a lot of fun.

10th July, 2018

Ameet towers, Mumbai.

Strangeness and then a lot of weirdness at the night. The party was over at half past 2, leftover cans with the coke in it and the plates were over the table. Balloons still looked good over the wall and the champagnes spill was still on the floor. Pillows were misplaced, and clothes were thrown. Wind hushed through the curtains and brushed my hair. Nothing was in its place after my 18th birthday bash and I was not drunk, my friends were. I saw 3 fucking pretty cakes on my party this time and they were HUGE. I sat on the couch of my balcony with a cigarette and my headphones. Everything was chill and cold. I got to remember *dilli ki thand (Delhi's winter),* which sounded like a dreamland. For a moment, my brain started functioning abruptly and I began to think something out of blue.

Is it like everything works according to the time. Is time everything? Do we really waste our time? Is time so precious? Is time everything.

If you ever feel timelessness, you might understand this.

From my school ages to my present life, I have been listening to one of the most common phrase that "Time is everything, don't lose it" or "The only thing that never comes back is time, so save it"

Well, I pretty much agree to the logic behind these overused phrases. Almost every successful men/women values time, they value it more than of dollars. Time is everything, it you lose it, it's just simply lost; you never have a time machine to get back and correct the things happened over past. Imagine you have a fancy time machine back in your garage and you got a chance to alter few things in the past, what would you like to change? Wait! Now this question might have some crazy out of box answers. Some would love to change their wives, while some would like to kill someone or do something else.

Well, what exactly is time? Is it something that had already been in the existence or is it something that is being introduced by us?

All corners of world had a different way to specify to time, the Chinese used to divide the day into 100 equal parts called 'ke'. The subdivision of hours and minutes into 60 comes from the ancient Babylonians who had a predilection for using numbers to the base 60. Our 24-hour day comes from the ancient Egyptians who divided day-time into 10 hours, they measured with devices such as shadow clocks, and added a twilight hour at the beginning and another one at the end of the day-time.

Interesting huh!

Its all man creation, hours, second and specific time specification. We live in a 24 hour world, we could have lived in a 48 hour world, if the time was specified in an other way by the men. We never loose the time, it's just the perception of what we are affected. For me there exists no time. I don't wish to lead my life according to hours and seconds but according to my body flow. I never know what's past and future but know what the present is. For me the definition of time is, what goes in present. But as to survive in this world you need to appreciate and follow the 24 hour time system, without this your life would just simply suck. Again time is really an important factor in everyone's life but I am more inclined towards the concept of timelessness. Everyone has their own definition towards the concept of time and that's pretty much appealing.

Dream

Do you think to be out of the box?

I always wanted to be different, I was a massy dreamer, I never stopped doing that, I dreamt of crowded hotel when I would be touring as a DJ or keyboardist, mob behind my Lamborghini and yeah bouncers dabbling themselves into the crowd and finally saving me. Girls sobbing with their friends when they just see me in massive concert. Populous costly air-ports, long black 2 seater Benz, good Gucci stuff and Calvin Klein time piece. I wish a private jet with winsome wine and wife on board; a white private cruise with all my booties in. Wanted a piano underwater and play it till sharks bit me in. Lend a rose to my future wife on the bluff when the sun shares its dead rays.

I dreamt of buying sun, the beauteous sun, but it's totally impossible. Wanna sit on the moon and gawk the craziness of world, follow the clouds, the unsecured white balls of laziness. Clouds teach a different lesson in our lives, it tells us to be free and unbound. Never let anyone to steal your ass. Be tender and dovey to all the men and women, sprinkle your love once in everyone's life, like it does by raining cold cold water on needy farmers who stare the calendar for the rain over the crops. On the other side of the page we see heavy lovers in the monsoon wrapping their lips with the smack of water and riding themselves crazier as the speed of rain accelerates. Smooth, sedate, seductive kiss in the rain! All nice and nude cloud looks elephantine spheres when looked from the earth but as we go upwards, we see it as flaky, light threads of silks or like as a mist. Crazy huh! Looks like something giant downstairs but when we take the elevator to the 100th floor we see the other beautiful side of it, scabrous and light.

Always wanted a *Latina* to marry, hang cute little babies with hazel blue eyes and a hook like nose on my back. I discovered that the babies have a part time job of crying and they never loose their job and keep themselves promoting.

Six

Smile, So It Streches Long As Nile

"And can I ask you a question?" Mrs Pallavi asks the backbencher

The backbencher (Aditya) looks befuddled and removes his square black James Jacobs glasses in a way that every actor tries to remove it. He stood up and adjusts his shirt a bit (A very common activity of every boy in a high school, i.e. to keep their one hand towards the back of the shirt, near the waist, to adjust it). He looks at the teacher and pretends that everything is all good.

"Yes ma'am!" he said in a confident way

"Am I joking here?" Mrs Pallavi scowls and slams her physics NCERT down the table. The class's noise level was almost reduced. All eyes turns towards Aditya, the stud of class X-A who is normally out in the Maths lesson and late to the class after the lunch break. His excuses are always mind-boggling, they are like, I didn't do my homework because I was on Netflix. BALLS BRO!

No! No one can be so dopey and say this reason to a fucking physics teacher but he was Aditya, he always tried to sound cool and real in front of everyone. He could have popped the most common excuse out that is, "Ma'am I actually did the homework but I forgot the notebook at home."

And then the teacher further asks, "*khaana khaana nahi bhule?"* (Didn't you forget to have your meal?)

"Why were you smiling and flashing those teeth off?" she asks Aditya

"Um. . . . . no! Ma'am" he utters and looks towards his bench mate.

"Well, get out!" Mrs Pallavi points towards the main door.

Aditya, the cool ass takes a 2 minute silence break, looks again to his bench mate and moves towards to the door. Principal office was his second home since last year, his parents were too bored to visit the school every time the complaint gets in. His dad was a millionaire and he had a stepmom who everyday packed him with mayo Russian sandwiches. Smokes and Bacardi was his everyday business. Well a brat!

"No shame is left in your pocket these days, directly marching off towards the door, no sorry, nothing!" Mrs Pallavi nearly drained out her energy and needed a break now.

Well this is the most common experience of a school life, Mrs Pallavi must have been in everyone's life with that scowl on the face. I normally used to point my enemy in the class and directly state him as the reason of my laughter. This was a normal classroom scenario of this century. Yes, he smiled and particularly he didn't commit crime, maybe the teacher wasn't teaching in a way that may pull out the attention of everyone or Aditya was smiling intentionally. Maybe he was smiling to his crush and she was smiling back, maybe he was grinning on his bench mate jokes or he found something zany in the physics concept that Mrs Pallavi took or something unusual scene from the Netflix series caught his eye.

OK so let me tell you that babies smile around 400 times a day and a normal happy person smiles 40-50 times and average of us just 20 times. I personally land in the third category and still lead a happy life though. I see fat people and women being more happier sometimes.

Why do we smile?

We smile because we shade positivity around our area, to our friends, family or to ourselves. Endorphins, dopamine are released when you smile and you finally feel blithe. You sit with a guy who smiles a lot and then who cries a lot, you will understand the vibe of each of them.

Sometimes you have a smile on your face because of a stupid act of your best friend, you smile when you end up doing a waggish activity in your neighbourhood, that maybe a making cut to your neighbour's T.V cable. You smile when you get to know about the new affairs between your school teachers or you get to know that the principal's car tire has been punctured by one of your friend. You grin when you end up setting trap for your challenger and then that finally works or sometimes you end up getting stuck in your own trap. Why do you smile though?

The most common phrase that arrived in the world is, "Smile is a curve that sets everything straight".

When your crush finally arrives to the class, a smile is set on your face. When the physics teacher is on leave you smile wider, and when you have two games period in a row, trust me there is no better day than it. There are ample of resources of what makes you like a dog with two tails sometimes. Well, I get a smile when my mom gets me my favourite meal i.e. rajma – rice with some extra curd or I get some extra pine-apple shake down the dusk.

A simple way to be in happy spirits is, do what you like the most, never be forced to do something you never liked. Never join PCM, if you paint unreal portraits like of Mona Lisa or never take commerce if you feel producing music like Bohemian rhapsody. Decisions play a major role in your life, like a major. Just like when the roots of your tree are strong, then the tree is said to be prominent. Don't let anyone, maybe your family, to take decisions of your life after you reach a matured age. Sitting into IITS and seeking into fat ass books might be your family decisions, not yours. Maybe your goal was to be a fashion designer and set the world into a refashion but you might be functioning your head in quantum physics or diving into some different concepts. Dream what you want to be and march to your decisions. You will end up being jovial, once you start working as per your choice.

Bring a smile on anyone you end up liking and make him/her on a cloud nine. Try to cook some interesting cuisine for your family and let your mom take a rest with a smile on her face. Feed a roadside beggar who might be living on a threads of wool, believe me, you won't be able to imagine their increase in the rate of happiness. You may also feed some of your extra milk to the cat nearby, who might thank you later by saying, "Meow, Meow".

When you try to make someone happy, you end up being happier. There are lots of people you're socially connected to, your girlfriend, friend, mom, dad, brother, everyone. Think of making any of them happy at any moment. Try going for a long walk with your bae and feed her with good thick humour. Feel like getting privileged to make someone smile and make their life smoother.

Everyone knows what they like and what they don't, make a list of what you like and pin over the wall or somewhere and try to follow that. Maybe an extra caffeine makes you happy or a Netflix series with a beautiful booty in it. A roadside *pani puri* with your bestie might turn you on or smoking some weed in the garage make you grin. A kiss over the terrace under the winking stars might turn up your best moment of life. There are millions of way to get happy or make someone happy, some are weird and some are common. Everyone turns to be happier with different reasons. You can't make everyone happy with a single act, some might refuse or hate it but some might extremely love it. So yeah making everyone smile is a backbreaking job, but you might see your mom doing it all right by keeping all the family members happy and delivering the needs of everyone; the reason she is said to be a god.

Never be scared of doing things that delivers you happiness unless its illegal. Don't be frightened to collect your own happiness if you feel that source of happiness might sound ghostly to anyone around you. If you like to serve in a café with those trendy blonde haircut, go ahead! Never try to listen the words, people end up saying, like in this case it might be that," Serving in a café doesn't make you earn good money and it might be regarded as a low category job but whereas in your perception it might be the other way around. You would possibly like to serve in a style that no one else does or would like to serve the elites and bring a smile on their face. Its all upon you what makes you smile. Break all the barriers you can and never work if you are forced too, you might bring on the depression in your lives. Your sources of euphoria might be frightening but you're trying make yourself happy at the moment not the others, just as I told, you can't make everyone happy with the same source.

Try to flash more teeth's than before, well, I didn't mean to ruin Mrs Pallavi's lesson. You get a different glow all over your face when you actually grin like a Cheshire cat. The muscles all over the face gets stretched and is termed to be a good exercise. People around, feel the attitude of optimistic over you, they try to spend most of the time and share some of the problems with you. Socially, you start to become more acceptable, you get more new homies to talk along. Making yourself and someone happy can make up your entire day sometimes. You might have noticed someone saying that,

"You know she has the best smile in our class" (I remember my friend whispering me this in the grade 9 when he was crushing over someone.)

"When he smiles, I feel my day has been completed." (This must be one of the common lines around the girls, maybe the phrase has turned a bit old.)

"You look good when you smile that way." (We were over the swings in a park and she cleverly caught my eye and said it.)

"I really love the way you smile." (We were laying over the terrace, looking at the nude clouds and over a couple of minutes I looked towards her and said it.)

"I feel empowered by your smile." (This might be a mom saying to his cute little boy, who never does bad things and keeps smiling all the day.)

"I love your smile more than you." (Well, I never heard this anyways!. This might be a more selfish situation.)

And finally, "Smile please! Or Say cheese!" (This is the most important aspect of smiling, without a smile the photographs wouldn't be alive and photographers wouldn't use this line.)

So keep smiling.

We find many ways to smile and should keep finding more to maintain the happiness

Seven

Lost, And We are Lost Once Again!

All lost, we all are lost, some of them in smoking joints, some in swiping Instagram stories, some in sipping Frappuccino's, some are lost in the woods, some in previous night's dream, lost in someone's smile, lost while watching a movie, lost while kissing someone, lost while driving on a freeway, lost in rain, lost in the darkness, lost in ensuing madness of the world.

How frequently do we get lost? Why do we get lost? Where do we get lost? How do we get lost? Are we lost all the time? Does someone makes us lost around? Is everyone around us lost alike us? Do we love getting lost every time? Does the source of looseness overpowers us sometimes? Do we feel happy after getting lost or it depends? Is being lost the way you like, becomes your ultimate *zaroorat (desire).*

We are lost, everyone is running around in circles full of circles, lost in different angles of our own galaxy. Somethings carries us far in their own world, so far away that we loose the hold over us and we loose like the threads of flaky white clouds. ***Some things takes couple of years for us to get lost, some few months, some a bunch of hours and some makes us lost in few minutes!*** Not in all the cases, but there are few sources of getting lost where you see the cars floating up and if you see a glass object, it seems to melt away in a smoother way. You reciprocate late to what other men or women are asking you to. Their words seem like the sin wave with the slowest frequency or in simple words you start living in the slo-mo world, your eyes start to turn heavier, the input and the processing signal of the brain catches some rust and you fill your body with slow breaths and with a nominal heart rate.

All metamorphose into sheeny,
The way you figure out things,
No roughness makes you worse,
Neither a cop, nor a dog,
Nothing then cozens you up,
Time keeps a state of calmness,
And you deal with your heart,
No rules halt you apart,
Green signal falls
And the red
Scares to take a call.

These are the common drug effects that you normally see after a good consumption

Well, back to the topic, what makes you feel lost. The answers to this question are different for each and everyone. Some are lost in producing music, or singing some classical top charts music whereas some are lost in dancing on the beats of Bollywood or on the Carnatic. India turns to be the next EDM hub, youngsters spend thousands to get the concert vibe, Why? Just to get lost in that kickass composition and the cheesy vocals. Music industry trust out to be one of the biggest industry around the world. Some loose themselves by painting a complicated art and on the other side they loose the audience in their Gordian art. Did you ever think, why a world-class painting is worth around millions? Well the sign of the painter does matter but on the other way it hypnotises the viewer on the way they think. The artist designs a particular art, and maybe the viewer would think in an other way, weird know?. Did you notice, that most of the things that makes you lost are damn expensive. Ex. Try to book a seat of the front row of Justin Bieber's concert, you will ruin your own bank balance but your moto of looseness on his billboard hits will be accomplished. We travel through many adventures to loose up completely.

Ever seen a stoner?

He losses himself everyday into space and that's an hard addict, sometimes you find them to smoke up twice a day, later on.

But if we see all the way around, there are two types of looseness, permanent and temporary. Stoners have to smoke up frequently to maintain themselves high.

Sometimes you are completely immersed in a Oscar winning movie but then it evaporates after some good time.

So these are like the temporary looseness for your soul, you repeat the action to get that same feeling all around the time. Energy consumption starts to become more at a greater rate. And the most important, something or the other becomes your *zaroorat.*

Try fading yourself out in permanent looseness, that may keep you the way you wanted all the time without performing the action repetitively. Activities like meditation, dancing or some music art can make you loose completely in your zone, you might not need anyone or anything to bring the excitement back. Tons of patience is needed to accomplish this act and a good amount of dedication and time. Some of them turn enlightened in their act and completely change their life.

Most of us do not like to try out this way and that's fair enough, world is way too fast. Everyone finds their own way to their den that brings the happiness. We are humans, we try to fade ourselves out, to bring some solitude, ecstasy or some good time. Some takes a good way and some, the bad. Well, nothing particularly can be calculated as the better or worse but still it must be taken care of before you bring the complete addictiveness.

Let's get lost together?

Eight

India

There used to be white beefy fog over the Delhi city and car's headlights and honks could only be figured out. I still remember my teenage diaries, when I used to drape myself with my mom's *kashmiri's shawl,* take some hot coffee over the terrace and then trip over the sunrise. Sunrise and sunset is the next level mojo all over. You go to Goa, you will see a different sunrise, maybe fly few thousands kilometres towards north India, Delhi and see a different phase of the sun. March towards Himalayas with some good looking fat jackets and check the sunrise down there; you will probably be blown out and build some positivity and dopamine content in yourself. I mean see this cosmic beauty of this nature that flips you up.

I love being an Indian, because if you get bored of living in the Northern plains with all the hurly burly of the metro city, you can always transfer yourself to the mountain region to check some bewteful Kashmiri girls and some highly priced apples; moreover if you are bored out with those monstrous, big mountains, you may take some time off to chill and relax in the beaches of Pondicherry and Goa. Maybe you can try figure out some good Thai spas there.

This probably defines the marvel of India. These many geographical features! Whoa,I have no reasons to escape India then!

In terms of types of food and fruit, India has never went down. If you are bored with the *pani puri* and *chole bhature* of *dilli,* try some crazy *vada pav* of Mumbai, that may gift your taste buds a good sapor and spice. Vada pav turns out to be a major snack of Mumbai. From students to employee or from a poor family to a richer one, a vada pav is sure for the day. Many of the sellers started earning in crores with the help of vada pav and gave a pause to the localities hunger. And sorry, I didn't tell you about the famous Pav bhajis of north India. Pav bhajis have always been a mouth watering street food. If you ever want to take your taste buds to a tour, believe me India gives you the best option. From *rasagulla (famous Bengali sweet dish) to famous paneer dishes* you find quite everything.

You find so many variants of complexion in India, which I think is pretty much a rare beauty hidden in this globe. Apart from this India is box full of language. Hovering over the state without even knowing the regional language might be a lot of fun and a disaster sometimes. Fly to a state which works with a language that is not registered to you and then try to communicate! Believe me, it might be one of the off wall or the craziest experience in your life. If you ever end up in a dispute, try to yell the opposite with your regional language that he must be unaware of and end up in ripping his ass. This is one of the tricks I usually follow to end disputes.

Do you know, a random word in your language might have a particular meaning and that same random word will figure out a different meaning in an other language.

Now wait! That random word might be treated as an appropriate word in your language but not in the other. Imagine yourself saying a random word that might be applicable in your language and might turn out a slang in other! Well, that's the weirdness of multiple languages. You never know that when you would turn up saying something weird to someone. India is pretty known for its traditional Hindi language but nowadays the trend is changing towards the fancy English. Now parents are never interested to make their kids learn Hindi, they feel English determines their status. Kids with 2 front teeth are trying to speak broken English. I mean its fine that a universal language should be maintained and you must be well versed with it to fly around the globe, but at the same time it doesn't mean that you loose the connection with your traditional language. Almost 70% of Indians are comfortable with language *hindi,* but still they use English to protect their standards and status. India's pretty famous and known for its multiple languages. Outsiders try to show their interest towards language *Hindi* and try to learn it. We should anyhow protect and carry forward the culture of our *Hindi* language.

What else, I mean India is a great land. You find pretty much everything that you may or may not discover in the world. Never attacked a country, it was always friendly to let others attack. You see the number of babies India produce everyday; is at the next level. If you ever become a celebrity or a cricketer, basically you shouldn't be on tenterhooks for a good crowd. Bollywood actors are treated as god here; ever saw the crowd roaring in front of legend *sharukh khan's* house?

Well, if you ask me, India is a maze in itself. You might figure out any type of *jugaad* and *jugaadus* here; not every country can afford this.

Nine

What's that perfect 'sēzən?

A thick woodland bright coloured jacket with snuggly pockets, a warm comfy jogger with a pair of white converse kicks, a warm smile over you to keep your body warm, and a cup of *kadak chai (Indian Tea)*. Well, winters is not just a season with few months in the year but a good time for the teenagers to show of their wardrobe. Winters turn everything patient and unfazed. If you ever want to seek *shanti* (peace) in your life, wish yourself to sit in the Himalayan region and then feel free to turn yourself as a saint.

My alarms used to snooze endlessly and then mom was the only solution in my life to wake me up for the school. The only trick she would ever apply to wake me up was to switch off the fan of my room. Believe me! This ruffles your feather and you start getting off the bed in particularly no time.

Winters and monsoons months turn out to be one of the sluggish months of the year. Bonfire, a good rum and a warm sweater might turn your life happier. In my school life, I used to wait for the winters to drop in, because it helps you to wear good formals with a blazer in the school. Mellow sunshine and sweet corn always succeeded to make my day better. That's what winter is all about; warm kisses, laughter and good food.

Like wise Winters, we have few more seasons down the line. Every season depicts something deep. Winters tells us how to grow with patience and calmness or how the life can be really paralyzed when nothing works out particularly.

Well, what about the *summer aura?*

(I remember diving into the swimming pool and then crying for a help!)

For me I would relax in the beach with a glass of lemonade and rubberneck to some booties on my view (*Besharam*). Would love to wear good tropical shirts and party with some good deep house music. Summer headways itself in a good time. You always have a bunch full of holidays when it comes to summer season. Well, taking a break from the hustle of the town, with files full of work is always a better choice. It peps up all your sense back. Moreover in this season your washing machine is not so overloaded as of winters. The most important thing is that, we try to hydrate our body to the core. Summer makes us to travel, relax, explore, breath in some fresh air and helps to put on some good Louis Vuitton shades.

Hold on! I have a foremost reason that why *summer* is my favourite, and that is it brings the festival of colours (*Holi*) with it, and hitting water balloons from the balcony over the bald head scooter drivers is a *cake full of fun.*

The Summer!

A bright sun cruises the sky,
I smile in a way that brushes my soul,
Everything turns so zappy and great,
She turns her skin chocolaty,
Smooth as caramel,
And then the late lost city wind nudges on me,
The jazzy birds play the rhythm of life,
I feel so crisp baked,
That I end up widening my long lasting smile,

How You Imagine Yourself In Aûtumñ?

I lust after her curved smile,
Hope is molt as of dried leaves,
Wait, I see the threads of colours in the sky,
I soak my eyes to the grizzled bewteful maple faced leaf,
The entr'acte turns ere long,
I live in the dingy whiff,
I say to the god,
Gift me her spring smile back.

We then wait for the spring to swoop in because it allows you to play with some garden fresh air. Life is like seasons, sometimes full of blissfulness, just like the spring time or its like an autumn when butter of dolefulness dives into your life. Its all about how you get a buzz out of every season of your life and lead it further.

What's That Perfect 'Sēz n? Part II

OK so, ever paused for a right time. Did everything in your life took place at the right moment or not? Are we so patient to wait for the right moment ? Well, I don't sometimes. Maybe I take the moment and make it right? Um, not so advisable every time.

Is 18 the right time to do all the bad things? No! That's not true.

You never get things you always crave for!

Ever thought about it.

Well sometimes the statement turns true but not at all the times. It totally doesn't mean that the dream you must be craving for, doesn't turn true. But what exactly makes that dream turn true?

The perfect season makes it all true. You count the days for a perfect season to arrive and then the fruit is yours. If you never wait for the perfect season you might end up in getting just small bud. Now it's all up to you that whether you wish for the perfect moment, pluck the fruit and enjoy its richness or whether you turn up to get the bud of a plant!

To be honest we just need a super quick output for everything, we sometimes forget about the road to be taken, sometimes the road to be taken turns wrong and sometimes it turns to be good. We often turn our patience level to the floor and choose shortcuts in our life to make things alive. But always remember these shortcuts never sustain longer in the lifespan.

Ever thought that what makes you far from maintaining a good patience balance? Why do we lose our string of patience over a period of time. Is it normal? Or its just something else.

We tend to loose our patience as we keep in trying to think of a considerable output but never for the process. You think of an end output or maybe the ultimate success for the longer time, you end up loosing your shit i.e. patience and get distracted from the process to reach your ultimate goal. Its all about, how you wait for the right time to proceed in and then hit a shot. Now, when it comes for the right time, the result always turns to be worthy and delightful. If you ever feel misplaced over time or feel lost like a nomad, try strengthening your process, feel concentrated and hit the shot.

To ever achieve the goal you always wanted to hit, try to build the stamina to sustain for so long and to stumble of all your barriers. The moment you try to forget of being succeeded and try to devote yourself more on the process; you build up a better chance to eat a sweeter fruit.

Ten

Ok! Whats that Permanent?

I pretty much remember that yesterday's sunset was one of the most bewteful of ever I have seen. Dude! Today's coffee was the best! Damn! Nice Benz. Oh fuck! Look at that sky high building. Louise vuilton and some Gucci is what makes my life. Bro! You gotta good apple accessories. Oh wow! A mirror selfie with iPhone X.

Whoa! You flipping on those Nike sneakers. Congrats! You gotta new G shock watch. Whoop! I got loads of dollars. Hey! You looked arousing when you stripped down in that red dress! Last night's pizza was mouth watering!. Whoa! I heard your dad got you a Harley Davidson last week.

Yes! We live in an artificial attractions and we eventually love to. Running in a race to compete others for the fleek accessories. It's never wrong to develop a fashion or to look attracted but on the contrary it doesn't lie in a pretty permanent stage.

What stays permanent turns temporary! You live today, you may die the next day! (Strange right!) Yes! ***The world is a strange machine, it never stops, it doesn't turn old; something makes an off the cuff move over the period of time.*** Something or the other cycles around somewhere, nothing ever stays the same. You might figure out the glorious sunshine with a good vitamin D today and see the thunderstorm the next day. You might see the sun rolling over the northern plains and see the glacier melting over the stack of hours.

Can I ask you a question?

What stays permanent in your life? Well, your mood?

You smile, then you might roll tears. You frustrate, then you might burst into a big laugh.

Your family, food, long sleek car, a furnished house with a good looking bathroom, thick cash, gold watch, few pairs of converse sneakers or like a room full of fancy trendy Gucci clothes?

Well, do you think is the luxury permanent? I don't think so. But no one takes a step back to refuse this snazzy flavour of lifestyle. We need four black cars with black windows instead of two, need a large pizza with the cheese burst when the requirement is still for a small pizza. We pull of ourselves towards the plush lifestyle. Nowadays we go to the Starbucks, well not to have a good palate of coffee but to improve our Snapchat and Instagram life. Weird? Or very Weird?

Well, according to me, I prefer a luxury taste to my life for a good amount of time but the fact is it ain't permanent! At some point of my life, I would have to filter this snazzy life of my region and that's the truth! Nothing stays so long, it comes and goes, comes and goes. All I can do is just witness what keeps going on.

Life is like a swing, it makes us go back and forth!

Now listen!

What makes situations good or bad? Do you make it or they are already a one!

Or is it because of the reaction you make after the action, makes the situation good or bad? What if there's nothing called a bad time! Everything is all good and perfect, nothing is out of shape. Life would be so normal, that it wouldn't be worth living.

What if everyday you wake up, it turns out with a good coffee and a forehead warm kiss, your meal turns good, your pop jockey undergarment shines off better and you might have a good glass of wine with a cool funky jazz in the background. But wait! Is that permanent? Making yourself happy all the time. NO! Things might change overtime, life may flip you like a skateboard! ***An action may change everything***, a day can change up the complete attire of your life. Ex- you might roll your wallet with loads of cash and good looking cards down the city (Well, this has happened with me!), and what if a famous rock band hovers over your YouTube videos and calls you for a world tour, what if your friend is murdered the next minute or what if you turn up making a suicide note, and what if a supermodel asks you for a marriage ?

Life turns out to be a crate of good and bad surprises, you never know when you unbox which surprise and then deal with it, you just have to build a good amount of patience. Nothing out stays there permanent, neither the good nor the bad. Never feel too depressed when something bad rolls apart and out of key, things just never turn out to be permanent. Nothing ever stops, things keep on rolling. Nothing freezes!

Well! And are you a permanent soul?

Even when you talk about yourself, you keep on rolling over many years to gift yourself many births. Enlightened are the ones who stop taking births and freed themselves from this role play of living in the so called ***life***. Well, talking about the enlightened, they contribute a good amount of patience to reach their destination.

Life is all about choices. The better you choose, the better you live.

So yeah, ***mark a brilliant choice.***

Thoughts

- ***Sail with your boat, go with a flow, a bewteful island will be always waiting for you.***
- ***Make yourself so big, so that other try to settle with you. Take time for everything.***
- ***Live with them who allows you to tell them your folk tales.***
- ***Flow is what needed in life, don't try to fade away.***
- ***Your determination level should be so high that even if your car gets punctured in the middle of the highway, you are anyways enthusiastic to reach your destination.***
- ***Sometimes uneducated teach the educated.***